WORKMEN'S HALLS AND INSTITUTES
OAKDALE WORKMEN'S INSTITUTE

BY GERALLT D. NASH, T. ALUN DAVIES, BETH THOMAS

AMGUEDDFEYDD AC ORIELAU CENEDLAETHOL CYMRU
NATIONAL MUSEUMS & GALLERIES OF WALES
CARDIFF 1995

First Published in 1995
© National Museum of Wales
Cathays Park
Cardiff CF1 3NP

ISBN: 07200 0430 6

Production: Arwel Hughes
Design and pre press: Ferguson Cowie
Type: Baskerville 10 pt
Printing: HMSO

Preface

In 1907, the Tredegar Iron and Coal Company started work on a new coal mine and 'model village' at Oakdale, Gwent. Ten years later, a purpose-built Library and Institute was opened in the village centre - a building that was to serve as a focus for the social and cultural life of the community for many years to come. The building of the Institute was financed through a loan from the Company, a debt that took the miners of Oakdale decades to repay.

The Institute contained a library, reading room, and committee room, as well as a concert hall which occupied the whole of the first floor. A separate, but linked, billiards room was housed in a building behind the Institute, on top of which was later built a larger public hall *cum* cinema. These buildings were used for concerts, eisteddfodau, political meetings, lectures, pigeon and poultry shows, dances, miners' lodge meetings, as well as providing venues for local clubs and societies ranging from the Women's Institute, Chess Club, St. John's Ambulance and Debating Society to the local Dramatic Society and Silver Band.

Following the demise of the coal industry, the Institute went into decline and finally closed its doors in 1987. Two years later it was dismantled and transported to the Museum of Welsh Life, where it has now been refurbished to its appearance in the late 1930s. However, the Museum's intention is not to display the Institute as a lifeless exhibit, but to use it as a venue for activities in keeping with the spirit of its original function. The aim of this book is to set the Oakdale Workmen's Institute in its historical context, drawing not only on written sources and photographs, but also on recorded interviews with some of Oakdale's residents.

The First Miners' Libraries

The dramatic expansion of coal mining in the south Wales valleys during the second half of the nineteenth and early twentieth centuries resulted in an unprecedented growth in population; that of the Rhondda valleys, for instance, soared from 4,000 in 1861 to 163,000 by 1891. Complete new towns and villages appeared along the narrow valleys where the coal seams were most accessible. The nature of the topography dictated the ribbon-like developments of terraced housing which were cheap to build, and created instant communities of people sharing the same place of work, religion, aspirations, co-operation in times of hardship, and grief in times of tragedy.

With the building of thousands of terraced houses in the south Wales valleys, it was soon realised that other facilities were required such as shops to help feed and clothe the population, and chapels to 'feed' their souls. Speculators and entrepreneurs erected many buildings including hotels, lodging houses, and public houses. Even so, most communities still lacked social and educational amenities. It was only in the older tinplate and iron ore towns, found at the edge of the coalfield, in places such as Gorseinon or Tredegar, that there were any established community facilities in the form of Mechanics' Institutes, Temperance Halls and Literary and Scientific Societies.

Elsewhere in Britain, attempts had already been made by some industrialists to provide such facilities for their workers. This arose out of a desire to create a reliable and stable workforce, and a wish to combat intemperance and drunkenness that had become the hallmark of mining communities brutalised by harsh working and social conditions. Industrialists in Lanarkshire, Scotland and the north-east of England were the first to provide reading rooms and libraries for their workers during the 1830s and 1840s.

A government Report of 1844 describes the Govan Colliery Reading Room as being '... open every evening ... furnished with a long reading table and ... well lighted and warmed ...'; a worthy substitute therefore for the tavern, alehouse or public house for the colliers of that area. Their recreation had, up to that time, been based on the cock-fighting, bull-baiting, pig-fighting and dog-fighting pursuits of the previous century, often accompanied by hard drinking, violence and domestic and industrial distress. The establishment of more civilised pastimes therefore served both the humanitarian concerns for a family's welfare and the desire to increase coal production and stabilise the workforce. Non-licensed clubs and tea-rooms had also been established during the middle decades of the nineteenth century, deliberately sited away from the nearest source of alcoholic refreshment. These, in parts of the north of England, grew alongside the early reading rooms and libraries.

Noble though these ideals and attempts were, however, there is little evidence to suggest that they were particularly successful. A Commissioner's Report of 1850 states that in Durham and Northumberland, where reading rooms and libraries were opened following the strikes of 1839 and 1844, the facilities '... were very little used and have in some cases been abandoned...'. The experiment had proved to be insufficient to divert the minds of the majority of English miners away from other pastimes. The minority that had joined the reading rooms had been, in most cases, insufficient to keep the premises open as going concerns. A good number were therefore closed, along with the temperance institutions that accompanied them.

Miners' Libraries and Reading Rooms

The second half of the nineteenth century, however, witnessed a dramatic change in fortune for the reading rooms and libraries founded during that period. These were to be followed by a boom in the building of the large, recreational Institutes that were to play such an important part in the life of miners. No single factor can be credited for the establishment of these new reading rooms and libraries which flourished in the coal mining areas, and particularly in the south Wales valleys, but Foster's Education Act of 1870 had gradually produced a working class that was capable of reading, a workforce that was, furthermore, eager to pursue its quest for knowledge. This, no doubt, was an important element in their foundation.

Before this, chapels were normally the only places where people could congregate for social or cultural purposes. Very often these led the way in fields other than religion. They were certainly the standard bearers of education for the masses in Wales during the early nineteenth century. Education was seen as a way of personal betterment and of improving one's prospects. Chapels, where collier and manager could meet on an equal footing, encouraged learning and literacy. Their Sunday Schools attracted tens of thousands of people each week to classes where young and old alike were taught to read and write, debate and discuss. Many also possessed their own libraries, though the emphasis was largely on theological subjects. These Sunday Schools have been described by one commentator as the 'greatest popular movement of the nineteenth century'.

The Games Room at Aber-Blaengwynfi Workmen's Hall, West Glamorgan (by courtesy of the South Wales Miners' Museum).

These chapel members and their leaders, both in the persons of coal owners and ministers, were to play an important part during the period from about 1875 to 1914 in the establishment of libraries and reading rooms, where books of a secular nature could be consulted along with the classics of the chapel library. The reading rooms and libraries and subsequent recreational Institutes were in the main paid for from a-penny-in-the-pound levy from wages which was matched by the coal owners. Joint committees of workers and officials were formed, premises secured, often in front rooms of houses or back rooms of shops. One of the earliest one-roomed venues to be established in South Wales was at Cwmaman in the Cynon valley in 1868, a reading room being added in 1871 and expanded further in 1884 when it moved into two-roomed premises consisting of both a reading room and bagatelle room. This was the forerunner of the larger, recreational establishment that was to follow. A paper library was soon established, furnished with newspapers, journals and periodicals. A similar pattern was seen at Ferndale in the Rhondda Fach valley, where a reading room and library were established in the High Street in 1884.

The miners of the Maindy and Eastern collieries contributed a levy from their wages which was more than matched by one of the most benevolent of coal owners, the industrialist David Davies of Llandinam. In this instance, an initial payment of five shillings (25p) was obtained from each collier and timberman and three shillings (15p) from labourers and hauliers. Small, fortnightly contributions were then secured. A site was secured at Tonpentre for £1,000 and an ambitious project undertaken which illustrated the success of co-operation between the owner and worker for mutual benefit.

The published catalogue of the contents of the Parc and Dare Institute Library in Treorchy provides a fascinating insight into the diversity of the subjects covered, which may be summarised thus:

General Fiction	360	books
Poetry	47	
Biography	100	
Sociology	78	
History & Travel	82	
Essays	55	
Theology	77	
Music	16	
Miscellaneous, including Reference	88	
Yr Adran Gymreig (Welsh section)		
Nofelau, Barddoniaeth, Drama (novels, poetry, drama)	56	
Bywgraffiad (Biography)	30	
Llenyddiaeth Gyffredinol (General Literature)	34	
Diwinyddiaeth (Theology)	71	
Hanesyddiaeth (History)	37	
Science	119	
Papers and Magazines		
Daily	9	
Weekly	30	
Monthly	13	

Following a visit to the library and reading room at Maerdy, in the Rhondda Fach valley, in 1892, a columnist for the Glamorgan Free Press wrote:

The room was crowded. On all sides could be seen the hard-worked colliers, with the characteristic rim of coal dust on the eyelids. A glance around the room showed me immediately the interest and earnestness with which each was devouring the contents of some book or newspaper...

This is the image that has been frequently transmitted of the early attempts at co-operation between owners and workers to not only promote knowledge by the establishment of centres of self-education, but also to create a more contented workforce that would better serve the community both socially and economically.

The impressive facade of Blaenafon Workmen's Hall and Institute, Gwent, photographed in 1980. This building has recently been refurbished as part of the government's Valleys Initiative.

Workmens' Institutes

Even though miners' libraries had become an important and increasingly popular feature of the Welsh mining communities during the late nineteenth century there remained a need for recreational facilities for the workmen and their families - places where they could meet to relax, attend concerts, lectures, dramas and compete in eisteddfodau, somewhere where clubs and societies could meet, where the local band could rehearse and perform and where pigeon and poultry shows could be staged.

A typical list of objects for the establishment of an Institute may be seen in the published *Rules of the Abertridwr Institute*, a document which resembles a social charter for its members and their welfare.

Established for the purpose of carrying out social welfare activities pursuant to the Friendly Societies Act of 1896, the objects of the Association formed to run the Institute specify that there should be provided:

(a) Circulating Library
(b) Reference Library
(c) Reading Room
(d) Rooms for Billiards, Chess and Draughts and other recreations
(e) Large Hall for musical, dramatic and other entertainment
(f) Lecture Hall
(g) Lectures and other entertainments
(h) Such classes and other facilities as may from time to time be desirable to promote the objects of the Association.

From about 1890, Miners' Institutes gradually became a feature of the south Wales valleys landscape. In order to accommodate a range of activities, as well as a library and reading room, these were often large structures, usually architect-designed, sometimes of considerable architectural merit, with their facades designed to impress even if the remainder of their exteriors were more mundane.

Many Institute buildings, such as those at Nant-y-moel (Ogwr valley) and Ynysybwl (Clydach valley), were chapel-like in appearance, but more elaborate facades were favoured in later buildings as in the restrained Classical facade of the Bedwas Hall and Institute (1923), or the 'Arts and Crafts' frontage of Ferndale (1909). Some were unashamedly civic in both design and scale whilst others (Aberbargoed, 1904, and Wyllie, 1934) owed more to the domestic scale of the vernacular revival movement and to the influence of architects such as Voysey. The front of Fforest Fach Hall was distinctly Italianate in style, the outside being rendered in white cement and with tall, arched pilasters and a pantile roof. The Cwmllynfell Institute, in contrast, was a severe modernist design of reinforced concrete with the facade punctuated by symmetrical rectangular window openings.

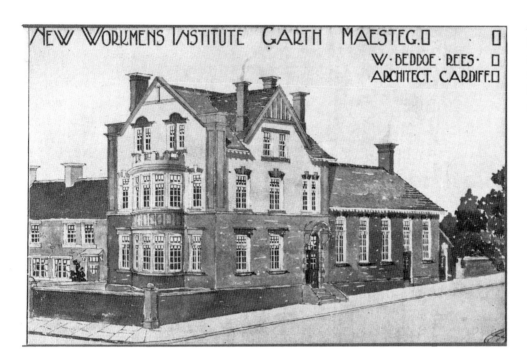

An architectural perspective of the proposed new Workmen's Institute at Garth, Mid Glamorgan, by the Cardiff-based architect, W. Beddoe Rees.

A good example of a smaller miners' Institute at Cefn Cribbwr, near Bridgend, Mid Glamorgan, photographed in the 1920s. As with most other Institutes, billiards was a popular attraction: several of the men in the photograph are holding billiard cues.

One of the earliest Institutes in south Wales was that built at Penrhiwceiber (Cynon valley), at a cost of £1,800. It was opened in 1880 by Lord Aberdare, the local coal owner. It contained a large hall (seating 600), a small hall, library, reading room, billiards room and a committee room. It was further extended in 1900. At Cwmaman, also in the Cynon valley, where workmen's reading rooms had been established in the 1870s, an Institute was opened in 1892. Unfortunately this burnt down in 1896, but just a year later a new Public Hall and Institute had been built, Lord Aberdare again officiating at the opening ceremony.

In many instances the finance for these projects took the form of loans from the local coal owners. However the Dinas Institute (Rhondda Fawr) was paid for entirely by the philanthropist Caroline Williams. This building, which cost £1,700 and which was opened in 1893, contained a 250-seat hall, library and separate men's and women's reading rooms. The Llanbradach Workmen's Hall (Rhymney valley) built in 1913, was similarly the result of a donation. Here, there was a large hall (capacity 1,000), library, reading room and billiards room. The Ystrad Institute (Rhondda Fawr) was paid for by Clifford Cory, the coal owner and industrialist. This building contained men's and women's reading rooms together with a library, magazine room, billiards room and a games room. Cory also paid for the Pentre and Tynybedw Collieries Free Library and Workmen's Hall (Rhondda Fawr) which was built in 1893 at a cost of £3,000.

The Ynyshir Institute (Rhondda Fach), opened in 1905 at a cost of £8,000, contained a large hall (seating 1,500), library, reading room, games room, billiards room, gymnasium and committee rooms. Another huge building was Nixon's Workmen's Institute at Mountain Ash in the Cynon valley. Erected in 1899 at a cost of £8,000, this contained a theatre (seating 1,500), lecture room, library, reading room, swimming baths in

Penygraig Workmen's Institute, Rhondda Fawr, Mid Glamorgan, nearing completion in 1910.

the basement, billiards room, gymnasium, games room and committee rooms. Even the local magistrates court and county court held their sittings there during the early years of the present century as there were no other suitable premises available at the time. Some Institutes even had branches in other towns or villages; Nixon's for instance had a branch library and hall at Penrhiwceiber for use by workmen from the Navigation Collieries who lived in that village, whilst the Tredegar Workmen's Hall had branches at Troedrhiwgwair and another at North End (1925).

Many of these early Institutes came about as a result of discussions between like-minded individuals, - generally colliers, but also including some colliery supervisors, and, occasionally, managers (sometimes on behalf of the owners). Initial meetings often took place in chapel vestries or in private houses where ways were sought to raise the money necessary to pay for these purpose-built Institutes.

The Miners' Welfare Fund

Following industrial unrest in the coalfield, the government set up the Sankey Commission in 1919 to look into the running of mines and miners' interests. One major and significant development resulting from this Inquiry was the establishment of a Miners' Welfare Fund, which would receive a penny from every ton of coal raised in Britain. Money from this Fund was used to finance the provision of new or improved facilities in existing workers' halls or, more significantly to help build new Institutes and Welfare Halls in those area

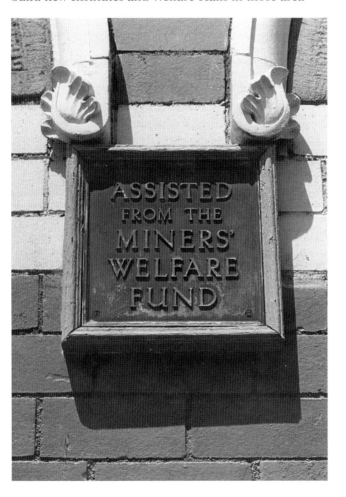

which had hitherto been unable to afford them. Thanks to the Miners' Welfare Fund, probably as many Halls and Institutes were built during the 1920s and 1930s as were built during the previous forty years, and by the Second World War south Wales had at least 135 Workmen's Halls, Institutes and Welfare Halls.

The Miners Welfare Commission, which administered the Fund, established criteria governing what could be supported:

> *... that part of the building (or the whole building) which is available for indoor games, including the reading room and library and committee rooms, one or more of which are usually regarded as necessary for the purpose of small meetings of various kinds...*

Many of the Institutes and Halls that were built or extended during this period also contained theatres, concert halls and, increasingly, cinemas. The cinema, especially following the arrival of 'talking' pictures, proved to be extremely popular and profitable, and projection rooms and screens were often added to attract more people.

Problems arose, however, as a result of the economic depression which followed the Great War, the industrial strife of the 1920s and the general decline in the numbers of both collieries and their employees. These had a profound effect on the viability of many Institutes. However, the various classes and societies which used these Institutes during the years following the great strike of 1926 kept going in spite of the daily hardship being endured by miners and their families. In 1928, the Rev. Samson Iles attracted between eighty and a hundred people to the Deri Institute to listen to a talk on 'The Pacific and its Wonders'. Dr. F. J. North addressed 250 at Trealaw on geology whilst the

Institutes and Halls which received financial assistance from the Miners' Welfare Fund usually displayed a plaque, as in this example at Glyncorrwg, West Glamorgan.

Abercarn and Cwmcarn Institute, Cwmcarn, Gwent, built in 1923: a typical example of the type of Institute built with money provided by the Miners' Welfare Fund.

Rev. Dyfnallt Owen addressed a smaller number at Llwydcoed and Cwmaman on literary subjects. The Rev. Philip Jones of Porthcawl's afternoon talk on 'The League of Nations and Citizenship' at Cefncoed-y-cymer that same year saw a full attendance as did a talk on 'Evolution and Religion' in the evening. The Rev. William Evans (Wil Ifan) addressed a full house at Llwydcoed on the subject 'Y Cymro'n canu' (The Welshman singing), and Dyfnallt Owen had a full house of 100 at the same Institute on the subject of the social reformer 'Jac Glan-y-Gors'.

The books housed in the miners' libraries covered a considerable range of topics, but the condition of the libraries themselves was frequently poor. At Tonypandy, there were 1,800 books, many worn, whilst at Penygraig the local colliery was in great trouble, and the library was described as being 'in a parlous state' with only twenty-one subscribers. At Ystrad, the library was well looked after by a competent librarian. In the neighbouring Cynon valley, Abercwmboi had a small library of 560 volumes which was considered very inadequate. The Aberaman Institute opened by

Keir Hardie MP in 1909 recorded 1,000 borrowers reading thirty-thousand books in 1928, but there was an urgent need for new volumes. A similar, uneven pattern was to be seen in the Merthyr Tydfil district where eight libraries housed 13,000 books for the benefit of a population of 90,000, but 90% of the books were of a pre-war date and in need of replacement. The author of the report into the Merthyr Tydfil district libraries, David E. Evans, stated '... It would be a blessing if, during these 'lean years' something could be done to save these great institutes, which contribute so much to the welfare of these mining communities...', but despite the provision of funds by educational bodies, local councils and charitable societies to replenish the libraries and reading rooms, particularly in the Rhondda Valleys' twenty-two libraries, the emphasis gradually moved from the provision of the literature to the survival of the Institute as a going concern. Ironically, and sadly, the peak of use of these libraries was recorded in 1926, when statistics show that there were tremendous increases in the borrowing of books, at Cymer Institute, for instance, from 29,238 in 1925 to 49,161 during 1926, 'the year of the long stoppage', which led the author of the Carnegie Report in that area, Brinley Thomas, to comment '... The extra time and mental energy at the disposal of the miners during these long drawn-out months of 1926 resulted in an abnormal boom in reading ...'. It was a boom that was never to occur again. The same writer noted that '... The heavy demands of mortgages, overdrafts and loans will be a first charge of the restricted income of many Institutes for years and the only libraries at the disposal of a population of 159,000 will become more dilapidated, out-of-date and curtailed'.

The Workmen's Institutes and Libraries served the whole community, at least in theory, though inevitably their management was largely in the hands of miners. As oral testimony from Oakdale confirms, children were generally discouraged, except for attending concerts or film shows:

When we were going to school... [the caretaker would] be standing on the door and he'd say "Good morning children. Straight past, don't come in here!" And we respected the place, you know...

Even though women's groups and societies made use of the facilities, they were seldom encouraged to participate in the running of the Institutes, other than in the more menial roles of cleaners, usherettes, or waitresses in refreshment rooms, as was normal for that period. The provision of reading rooms or libraries specifically for women, as at Dinas, Ystrad, Aberaman and Pentre, were indeed rare. Whereas women could become members of Institutes,- at Aberaman Institute for instance, by paying an annual subscription of 2/6 (12^{1}/$_{2}$p),- they were seldom represented on any committees. At Oakdale, the new Rule Book, produced following the transfer of responsibility of the Miners' Welfare Fund to the Coal Industry Welfare Organisation in 1952, included the following with regard to 'Lady Members':

... Lady members shall not be required to pay an entry fee and shall not be entitled to attend general meetings or vote at elections and shall not be eligible to hold office or propose or second candidates for office. They shall be subject to such special regulations as the Committee may from time to time make regarding lady members...

Only a handful of Institutes were built after the Second World War, one of the last probably being the small, utilitarian structure built at Ynyswen in 1961.

Nationalisation of the coal mines in 1947-48 brought extra funds for the maintenance of the Institutes and their libraries and the National Coal Board contributed generously to the refurbishment of buildings during the 1950s and 1960s. It is true that the main emphasis in many Institutes had switched to entertainment and money-making pursuits, but it should be stressed that the cultural and recreational functions of a good number of south Wales Institutes survived well into the last quarter of the century. The introduction of alcohol, the provision of live entertainment and the general inevitable drift towards money-making ventures essential to the survival of the Institutes changed the main character and emphasis of the 'Stutes, but survive they did as long as the pits remained open. With the demise of the south Wales coalfield and the closure of the coal mines, the clubs and Institutes declined and became mere relics of the social past of the industrial valleys. Many still exist but they have had to adapt drastically to meet the demands of the new valley communities. Many more have been demolished and merely remain as memories of the cultural and recreational activity that once existed under their roofs:

Like every other little place Oakdale 'Stute was the hub of the village. And it was the same in Tredegar Institute and the same in Crumlin, Newbridge, Abercarn, Ystrad Mynach and all around. Everything went on from there. But then it all went away from us and the miners didn't want to know... When the colliery closed it became a dead duck.

Oakdale: The Early Years

Oakdale village came into being in 1907. It was purpose-built by the Tredegar Iron and Coal Company to service the newly-opened Oakdale Colliery, and within less than twenty years it boasted an established community of more than 2,000 people, with well-planned housing, shops, places of worship, recreational facilities, a hotel, and, dominating the centre of the village, a Workmen's Library and Institute.

The Tredegar Iron and Coal Company had been formed by a consortium of wealthy industrialist families:- Maclaren, Markham, Pochin, Whitworth and Wyllie - who were all connected with coal mining. They decided to establish a new group of collieries in south east Wales with the aim of extracting coal primarily to meet the needs of the growing export market and negotiated mineral rights with the main land owners in the area.

The Oakdale Colliery, opened in 1907 by the Tredegar Iron and Coal Company, was one of the most modern and innovative in South Wales.

One area they chose was part of the relatively unspoilt Sirhowy valley. This was characterised by scattered farmsteads and cottages and the occasional nucleated group of buildings as at the cross roads at Penmaen where a Welsh Congregational chapel and the Cross Oak public house were located. Other buildings in the area reflected the largely self-sufficient nature of the small rural community; the workshop and dwelling house of Mr Rowlands the carpenter and, next to it, the house and workplace of the blacksmith, John Davies. South of Penmaen, towards Pontllanfraith, was located a water-driven corn mill, which gave its name - Melin ddŵr – to one of three terraces of houses built near the old Prince of Wales public house.

The work of clearing the site commenced in 1906 and the first shaft was sunk the following year. The second - the Waterloo shaft - was sunk in 1911, by which time plans were well advanced for building houses to accommodate the workers and their families. The new mine at Oakdale boasted the largest diameter shafts then found in south Wales. Trams of coal were lifted in double-decker cages to the surface giving the mine up to four times the winding capacity of some of the older collieries,- an important factor considering that the shafts were more than one third of a mile deep. Six of the eight coal seams were 1200mm (4ft) or more in thickness and two of them, named the Rhas Las and Polka, merged near the north shaft to produce a seam 2700mm (9ft) thick! Having struck such a fine, productive seam, the Tredegar Iron and Coal Company was able to offer higher wages than those paid elsewhere in the district.

The general pattern of housing in most south Wales mining towns had up till then been characterised by long terraces following the valley sides. Terraced housing represented an economical way of providing a large number of dwellings within the limited area available along the narrow valley sides. These linear, ribbon-developments became a characteristic feature of industrial settlements throughout the south Wales valleys, with the valley floors being occupied by the coal mines and their associated plant, engine houses and ancillary buildings, as well as the railways and roads which serviced the sites.

Alfred S. Tallis, J.P. (1863-1927), Managing Director of the Tredegar Iron and Coal Company, and one of the leading advocates of the Institute at Oakdale.

At Oakdale, however, a different approach was adopted towards housing the company's workforce. It was to be a 'model village'. The chief promoter of the project was Mr Alfred S. Tallis, Managing Director of the Tredegar Iron and Coal Company. He had the idea of combining a new, modern colliery with a new form of housing development that would be both attractive and stimulating to the workforce and would help attract workers to the new mine. The design for the village was prepared by Mr Tallis' brother-in-law, the architect A.F. Webb and land belonging to five farms were acquired for the proposed development. The new village was to be laid out in the form of a gigantic horseshoe with the main street running down the length of the village. Houses were laid out in the form of concentric crescents and avenues. At the centre was a formal lawned garden, where later a war memorial would be erected, on either side of which would be shops. Chapels, a school and a cottage hospital were included in the scheme, but dominating the centre of the village were two large buildings namely a hotel and a workmen's hall.

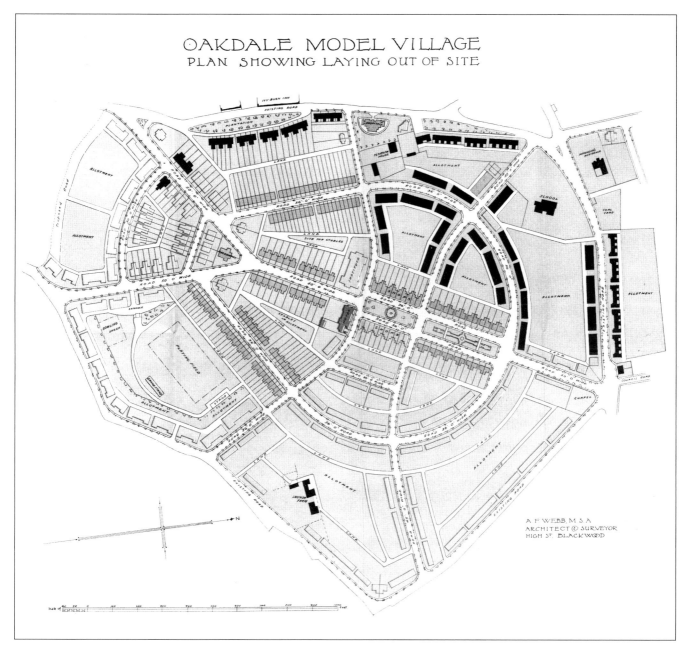

OAKDALE MODEL VILLAGE
PLAN SHOWING LAYING OUT OF SITE

Webb's master plan for the Model Village at Oakdale. Although there were slight amendments to the layout, the overall pattern of housing stayed true to Webb's original concept (by courtesy of Gwent Record Office).

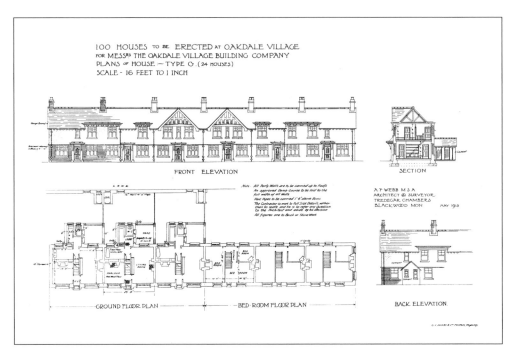

The 'Model Village' contained a range of house types arranged in short terraces and crescents. The architect, Arthur F. Webb, favoured designs which created interest and variety as illustrated by these drawings dated 1913 (by courtesy of Gwent Record Office).

A general view of the village centre, showing the Oakdale Hotel (left), the Institute, and memorial gardens in the foreground.

Webb's enlightened approach extended to the houses themselves. Each house was to have a large coal-burning range in the kitchen with an open fire on one side and a large oven on the other. A boiler was put into the back of the fireplace which heated water for the kitchen and the bathroom; this, at a time when bathrooms were considered luxuries in most workers' homes. It had been intended to provide every home with electricity supplied from the colliery generators but in the end only the colliery officials' houses in Penrhiw Terrace and one side of Syr Dafydd Avenue were connected to the service. A piped gas service arrived shortly afterwards but fifteen years and more were to pass before the remaining houses had electricity. Each house also had its own garden, and, unlike most terraced houses in the south Wales coal mining valleys, the houses did not face directly onto the street, but had a small lawned frontage between the front door and the street. The comparative luxury of Oakdale's housing was certainly appreciated by its residents:

[Oakdale] was a model village in a true sense of the word. It was years ahead of its time, because of the facilities, domestically. They didn't exist anywhere else. I mean, bathrooms for miners - Good heavens above!

Building work at the new village began shortly after the sinking of the first mine shaft, though initially the sinkers and construction workers were accommodated in wooden barracks nicknamed the 'Huts'. The school, begun in 1907-08, opened in 1909 and the first of the outer streets of the new complex - Syr Dafydd Avenue - was completed in 1912. This was followed by Penrhiw Terrace and Glanrhiw House - the colliery agent's residence - which stood opposite the school. Building materials were provided by the Tredegar Iron and Coal Company, including bricks which were made at the Company's own brickworks and transported to Oakdale by rail. The old Penrhiw farm was taken over and used as the residence of the chief engineer of the Colliery, beyond which was Penrhiw Terrace, a row of

eleven houses which were built for the colliery officials. Meanwhile, Birchgrove, Markham Terrace, Llwyn-onn Road and Ashville were completed.

With the onset of war in 1914, many young men left the mine to join the forces. However, the situation in Oakdale was not as acute as in other parts of the country. Coal was needed to fuel the war effort and mines were needed to produce it. Life must therefore have continued more or less as before, and, even though the effects of the distant conflict were felt from time to time when, for instance, a son or brother failed to return from the front, building work did not cease, and the expansion of the village continued. A row of shops and a post office, named Central Buildings, were built in the village centre at the top end of Central Avenue. But the most significant structure to be built during the war years was the Workmen's Library and Institute which, together with the Oakdale Hotel which it faced across Central Avenue, was to form the focal point of the village centre.

The Institute

The workers' barracks known as the 'Huts' had meanwhile lost their original function, and now served as a meeting house or hall for the emerging community. The first meetings of the local branch of the St. Johns Ambulance Service were held there, as were whist drives and meetings of the Women's Institute. By 1913, the employees of the Oakdale Colliery were meeting here on a regular basis and the Oakdale Workmen's Institute was formed. In that year also the first moves were made to establish a library there, and newspapers were delivered there daily. A rugby team had also been formed, though the Institute's Minute Book records that permission to use the library as a changing room after matches was refused!

The old 'Huts' which served as the workmen's Institute until the opening of the new building in 1917.

By the April 16th 1913 one of the rooms had been fitted out to serve as a games room, for which a billiards table had been acquired, players being charged 4d per half hour for its use. Billiards was to provide an important source of income for the fledgling Institute for several years. According to the Minute Book, on May 15th 1913 it was agreed that a chess board and pieces be purchased for 5/- (25p). Another room served as a reading room, with £1.18s.2d (£1.90) being spent per month on purchasing newspapers including the *Daily Mirror* and the *Daily Citizen*.

It soon became obvious, however, that larger premises were required. The billiards room was especially popular and members often had to wait for several hours for their turn at the table, and whilst the other rooms were suitable for small gatherings, there was nowhere (other than the school) where large numbers could be accommodated and hence there was little scope for community involvement in activities such as amateur dramatics, village meetings or even social events such as dances or 'magic lantern' shows.

On 20 August 1913 the possibility of a new Institute building was first raised by F. R. Webb, and on January 6th 1914 Mr Harry Blount, seconded by Mr Charles Hooper, proposed that the Committee should '...proceed with the New Institute at once...'. Mr Webb, who suggested the idea in the first place, was chosen as architect. It was agreed that the cost of the Oakdale Workmen's Library and Institute, as it was to be known, would be between £6,000 and £10,000. The scale of the challenge facing the Committee becomes apparent when the possible cost of erecting the building - up to £10,000 - is offset against its available funds at the time, for in April 1914 the balance in hand was just £99. 18s. 3d (£99.91), more than half of which had been collected as fees for using the billiards table.

The Tredegar Iron and Coal Company was involved from the beginning with the promise of a financial loan towards the cost of erecting a new building to serve as a Library and Institute. The contract was awarded to Richard Jones of Caerffili and a ceremony was held on Monday 3rd July 1916 to mark the laying of the foundation stones. Two stones were laid, one on either side of the main entrance door: that to the left being laid by Harry Blount on behalf of the workmen at the Oakdale mine; the other being laid by A. S. Tallis representing the Company.

As preparations continued for the eventual opening of the new building it was felt important that a set of Rules be drawn up to place the Institute on a more formal and manageable footing. To this end the Workmen's Institutes at Ynysddu and Tredegar were consulted and copies of their Rules obtained which would serve as a pattern for Oakdale.

A billiards room was proposed for the new Institute. This would not be in the main building, but in a separate, linked, flat-roofed structure behind the Institute. It was proposed that the cinema, when it came, would be built on top of the Billiards Room. By 1917 the committee was looking in detail at the sort of furnishings that would be required for the new Institute; for instance the Concert Hall would have six rows of plush chairs, with the remaining 300 being of plain wood and costing 3s. 2d. (16p) each. Three tables were purchased from a Mr. Sedger at Pontllanfraith at £3 each and two reading stands for newspapers for £8.

By June of that year it was reported that building work was falling behind schedule and the architect, A. F. Webb, was instructed to get the contractor to speed up progress, the date of August 7th having been agreed upon for the opening ceremony. On July 3rd a sub-committee met to formulate a set of Rules for the Institute. Included in the Objects was a statement that it should serve as "...The Means of Social Intercourse, Mutual and Moral Improvement, and Rational Recreation..." An advertisement was placed for a caretaker and librarian, at £3 per week and a billiards marker at £1. 10s. 0d (£1.50) per week. The Institute would be open from 9am to 10pm.

Mr. F. L. Davies, a Director of the Tredegar Iron and Coal Company was to be invited to open the new building with Mr. Oliver Harries (one of the Institute's Trustees) representing the workmen. Also invited were Mr. Charles Edwards MP, Councillor W. Richards, Rev. W. Rees and Rev. D. W. Edwards. On July 31st however the Minutes

Trowels used at the ceremony to mark the laying of foundation stones at Oakdale Institute, July 1916. (The mis-spelling of Harry Blount's name on the engraved trowel and foundation stone reflects the local pronunciation of his surname).

An invitation card sent to guests to the official opening of the Oakdale Workmen's Institute.

record that the opening date had to be postponed and a new date was agreed upon. This duly took place at 4pm on Monday 10th September 1917 with A. S. Tallis, Managing Director of the Tredegar Iron and Coal Company performing the ceremony in place of F. L. Davies who was unable to attend owing to illness.

The Institute building was two storeys high and had been designed to be in keeping and in-scale with the surrounding houses and shops. It was built of local coursed Pennant stone with the facade and window reveals detailed in white Portland stone. The back walls were cement-rendered. The roof was covered, not with Welsh slate as might have been expected, but in russett-coloured 'Lightmoor' clay tiles manufactured at Brosely in Staffordshire. All the floors, including the upper floor, were made of concrete, the ground floor being covered with oak blocks laid on pitch, whilst the main hall upstairs was finished with wood-strip boarding. The Entrance Lobby and Foyer were floored in terrazzo as was the landing to the Hall upstairs. On the ground floor an Entrance Lobby opened into a Foyer from which doors led, in turn, to a small office (used by the Caretaker and known as the Manager's Office) to the right. The next door led into the largest downstairs room, namely the Reading Room, which occupied more than a third of the total floor area. The Reading Room held copies of the *Daily Herald, Labour Leader, The Times* and *Daily Telegraph*, the last two being supplied by the Tredegar Iron and Coal Co., and by 1918 the committee had agreed to purchase 'magazine reading cases' for use in the room. Behind the Reading Room was a small room that was used for committees or society meetings, whilst on the opposite side of the Foyer the corresponding room was used as a gents' toilet.

Continuing in an anti-clockwise direction, the next room was originally described as a Committee Room, but this was later fitted out to serve as the Library. Indeed, so popular was this facility that by 1920 serious consideration was being given to printing 500 catalogues listing the books held. Between 300 and 500 books were being borrowed each month with members even being allowed to borrow copies of the *Encyclopaedia Britannica* for two days at a time if they so wished. The final room, with its doorway opposite that to the Reading Room, was used, at various times, as a magazine room, games room and finally as a committee room. Leading off this room was the Secretary's Office.

Directly opposite the main entrance doors was the staircase to the first floor which one ascended through a decorative archway flanked by two sets of pilasters. Deep plaster ceiling cornices, moulded dados and skirtings were formed around all the rooms and hallway. Pilasters and moulded panelling in the foyer completed the picture.

The first floor was dominated by the Concert Hall which occupied the full length of the building. At one end was a small stage, with the remainder of the room containing sufficient space to seat, it was claimed, 350 people. Two small (storage?) rooms at either end of the landing completed the accommodation on this floor. The Billiards Room as mentioned earlier, was in a separate building located directly behind the Institute. Access to this room was through the pilastered opening to the left of the staircase arch. The Billiards Room contained six tables and a small refreshment bar, with seating arranged around the walls.

Heating was provided by a coal-fired boiler located in a separate building behind the Institute from which hot water was piped to cast-iron radiators located throughout the building. The Institute also boasted its own electricity supply with a generator motor and accumulators being housed in an 'Engine House' behind the main building.

A Literary and Debating Society was established shortly after the building opened and dancing classes were introduced as a means of raising money to purchase a piano for the Concert Hall. The Labour College was granted the use of a room to run a social science class and a branch of the Women's Institute was established in the village, meetings being held in the Hall. In 1918 an eisteddfod was arranged following the success of a similar event held the previous year in the 'Huts', and which had in fact proved to be the most profitable venture staged by the Institute Committee.

Members using the newspaper lecterns in the well-lit Reading Room, 1945.

H.R.H. Prince Albert (later King George VI) visiting Oakdale Institute, January 16th, 1920 during a visit to south Wales in his capacity as President of the Industrial Welfare Society.

Between the Wars

Strangely, although opened in 1917, the events of the First World War do not feature prominently in the Institute's Minute Book, even though some eight hundred workers from Oakdale Colliery served in the armed forces. An application for the use of a committee room for distributing 'council potatoes' (presumably seed potatoes to be grown in allotments and gardens) was refused, although the use of the Hall was granted later for a Victory Ball.

To many people, the new Institute was a place to go to relax after a hard day in the mine, with games proving to be a particularly popular attraction. Dominoes, draughts, and later, chess, were purchased for use by the members and by 1921 it was suggested that one of the rooms be designated a Games Room. In 1923 seventy whist tables were purchased, suggesting that the Hall was used to accommodate the two hundred or so people who might have taken part in a whist-drive. In October 1920, the first open show of pigeons, poultry and rabbits was held in the Hall, the proceeds going towards the local war memorial fund. But

The Billiards Room was located behind the main Institute building and was to prove one of its most popular attractions.

billiards was the most popular attraction, and the most profitable, though moves to turn the Reading Room into an additional billiards room were rejected. Within three years of opening the Institute the tables had to be re-covered at a cost of £170, a move that was welcomed by one member at least, for in 1922 J[ohn] Cable won the Welsh Amateur Billiards Championship for the third consecutive time. The Billiards Room proved to be an irresistible attraction and focal point to many generations of young men from Oakdale, as a former resident testifies:

I must have been about twelve when I first went in to play snooker. I was hooked and I've been playing it ever since, not to a great deal of proficiency, but with a great deal of enthusiasm... I remember how thrilled I was to have my own cue hanging up in the Billiard Room with a lock on the case. It was a great feeling to go across and bring your own cue out instead of having to borrow somebody else's. That was really something special... There were some very important matches there, because Oakdale had a good billiard team and a good snooker team... I've stood there and watched exhibitions for hours with some of these people and they were really very good at it. We queued for our game and we waited perhaps an hour and a half before you could get a table for yourself. And in the meantime while you waited you sat around the walls watching the others playing, through the smoke... But it was a great cultural place to be because discussions were raised around the table, of course. They weren't all about snooker, everything went on... I mean these men worked together and so you had the conversation about that going on around the table. And politics, of course... but you remember listening in awe as these men, learned men, discussed the affairs of the day. That was what the snooker hall was about...

The Committee worked hard to maintain standards in the Institute, but problems such as gambling and indiscipline did arise from time to time. In 1919 snooker pool was banned, and when chess was introduced, in 1924, it was on the understanding that it would be played in the Billiards Room '...as a means to improve order...'. The playing of cards had also been allowed, but this was banned (in 1925) '...owing to gambling...'. In fact, the situation deteriorated to such an extent that the Committee felt it necessary to appoint a person for two evenings a week, at 10s. (50p) '...to take charge and restore order in the games room...'.

The Hall was in great demand for concerts and meetings, and in 1919 footlights were purchased for the stage. Although some Sunday School classes were held in the building, a request that the Hall be used as a temporary place of worship was refused. The local miners, on the other hand, were granted the use of the Hall to hold a meeting to discuss the question of pit-head baths and the implications of nationalisation. The local branch of the Ambulance Brigade also made use of the building and in 1924 they were granted permission to have their own storage cupboard there. They had earlier won the A. S. Tallis Cup which was put on display in the Institute. The success of the annual Eisteddfod, on the other hand, was short-lived for in 1922 the idea was abandoned through lack of interest.

If the village of Oakdale had been cushioned against the full effects of the Great War, it could not escape crises in the coalfield. The General Strike of 1921 brought coal production in South Wales to a standstill and in that year Oakdale suffered its first strike. By April 12th that year, a 'Distress Committee' had been formed and a fund established to help miners' families who were suffering hardship. The Institute donated £10 to the Distress Fund. The cessation of mining meant that no wages were brought home and this in turn had a direct impact on the moneys received by the Institute. In April the billiards charges were reduced by a half, and snooker was, likewise, reduced, to a penny a cue. By July, the dispute at the mine had been settled, though the miners had first to agree to a drastic drop in wages. This in turn led to a reduction in the salaries of the Institute employees, as their wages were based on those of colliery workers.

Even the Brass Band suffered! In 1925 it had gone on tour to raise money for the strikers' fund, but the exercise had left it financially crippled. Many families found it difficult to pay the weekly house rent which, over the years had risen with the wages since 1912, but had not fallen with the wage cuts. The lower-paid men were often forced to give up their homes and share lodgings with people in the same predicament so that their combined wages could meet the one rent.

By May the following year, the entry charge to the dances was reduced to 2d (1p) for men and a penny (1/2p) for ladies, and the sum of £5 was donated to the 'Relief Committee'. Newspapers that had backed the coal owners during the dispute were withdrawn from the Reading Room. Even though the strike was effectively over by mid-May, its effects were still to be felt in December. Loss of earnings had caused real hardship for many families and it would be many months, if not years, before some loans and debts were paid off. This may have been the reason that one of the rooms was made available for a boot-repairing scheme.

Members photographed outside the Institute, 1920s.

23

The 'Picture House'

Throughout the first ten years of its existence the Committee worked hard to maintain the building in good order and to carry out improvements when the opportunity arose, and when cash permitted. In 1923 the interior was repainted and the following year the electric lighting was improved, and a decision taken to install a telephone. The floor of the Concert Hall was showing marked signs of wear and tear by 1924, and in March of that year the small stage was extended,- presumably to make it easier to accommodate dance bands, concert parties or choirs. Two years later a piano was purchased from Heaths of Cardiff.

However, the one facility that the centre lacked, and one that was becoming increasingly popular in the neighbouring towns, and indeed throughout south Wales, was a cinema. As early as October 1920 a suggestion had been made to convert the Hall into a Cinema, as it was felt that this would '...be a great source of revenue and a benefit to the village...'. The Committee, however, decided against the idea, presumably as it would have meant the loss of the only sizeable hall and place of assembly in the village. There were, however, strong rumours circulating in the area that there were moves afoot to open a private cinema in Oakdale. This would undoubtedly have had a detrimental effect on attendances and income at the

The New Hall (opened in 1927) was considerably larger than the original Institute building. It was later adapted for use as a cinema.

Institute. The Committee meanwhile received assurances from Mr. Tallis that he would '...do his best to prevent any private concern [from] building a cinema at Oakdale...'. When, in February 1923, an application was received '...from a Blackwood gentleman...for the letting of the Hall for two night picture shows...' it was, as might be expected, turned down. However, it did highlight the need for such a facility in the area and hastened a decision to build a large hall-cum-cinema on the site adjoining the Institute.

The first suggestion that the Committee should consider building a larger hall came just two years after the Institute was opened. Initially the project was to comprise of a swimming bath and a large hall. The architect, Mr. Webb, pointed out that costs had trebled since the tenders had been received for building the Institute just two years earlier and so it was decided to concentrate on the hall. Webb, for his part, informed the Committee that it would be necessary to increase members' contributions in order to cover the costs, not only of the new hall, but to pay off the balance on the original building. It was hoped that some funding might be forthcoming from the Miners' Welfare Fund. By April 1923, £1,200 was available for building the New Hall, which the Trustees felt was now 'absolutely necessary'.

In 1925 the New Hall came a step nearer. Mr. Webb was instructed to prepare detailed plans for a building to seat 650 people together with a stage and gallery, the cost to be £7,000. A suggestion that the scheme should include lock-up shops on the ground floor was turned down. In March it was decided that the new building should be a public hall rather than a cinema. Eight firms submitted tenders for the work of erecting the New Hall, that of Theo. Matthews of Fleur-de-Lys being accepted at £8,106. 17s. 6d. (£8,106.87p). The contract was to last twelve months and work was to start immediately. There was to be no ceremony to mark the laying of the foundation stone. The Miners' Welfare Fund were approached for assistance but the response was not encouraging. The Bank Manager, similarly, '...took a very pessimistic view of the whole concern...', fearing, correctly as it turned out, trouble in the coalfield. Even the Co-operative Society, who had proposed a loan of £2,000, withdrew their offer. The only assistance that was forthcoming was from the Tredegar Iron and Coal Co. who advanced loans which enabled them to maintain payments on the building of the New Hall and to purchase a house for the caretaker.

In order to increase revenue it was decided to increase the charges for meeting rooms in the Institute by between 25 and 50 per cent. A move to increase billiards prices was defeated but dancing classes were increased from 6d. to 9d. On April 23rd 1926 it was decided that the New Hall should be called the Oakdale Workmen's Hall. Eventually, on 17th August 1926 the Miners' Welfare Fund agreed to give a grant of £2,500 towards the New Hall.

Arrangements for incorporating a cinema in the New Hall proceeded apace. A decision was taken to purchase a *Power No. 1* projector on hire purchase and to build a projection booth at the back of the Hall. A trial screening was arranged for the Committee with a matinee performance on the following Monday for school children. November 2nd 1927 was chosen as the new date for opening the Hall. The first film to be shown was *'April Showers'*. A boy, D. L. Jones, was appointed Assistant (projector) Operator at 5s. (25p) per week, and three girls were employed as attendants at 12s. (60p) per week, dresses and aprons being provided by the Institute.

Everything that went on in Oakdale was in the Lesser Hall - concerts and choirs and everything. And then they built the Picture House. It was a fine place the Picture House. If you didn't go early on a Friday and Saturday you wouldn't get in. It was the best thing that happened to Oakdale because before that we had to walk to Blackwood... to pictures and things like that. But Oakdale Picture House was a godsend.

The interior of the New Hall or 'Picture House' viewed from the stage. The projection box can be seen at the back of the gallery.

On Sundays, the New Hall was made available for use by the Wesleyans as a temporary place of worship for a period of three months. In 1928 the Committee agreed to purchase a set of scenery from London for £15. 10s. (£15.50) and also decided to engage a small orchestra who would provide suitable backing music for the silent films being shown in the New Hall. The Institute was not only popular with paid-up members but also, increasingly, with non-members, so much so in fact that it was decided '...to ban them from all facilities - even the telephone - until they became members...'.

The outstanding balance on the Institute and New Hall was still considerable; in April 1928 it was more than £8,000, and whilst the latest popular films such as 'Barbed Wire', 'Charley's Aunt' and 'Beau Geste' were drawing the crowds, it was necessary to dispense with the accompanying orchestra just two months after being appointed. However, as some sort of accompaniment was a necessity in an era of silent movies, Madame Templeman was appointed Musical Director of the Picture House the following year.

Mrs Templeman would be there playing, and there'd be no speaking, it would just come up underneath like Pobol y Cwm do. She'd be there playing, wobbling on this old piano stool. But we could never understand why you had to have music playing while the picture was on. You were trying to watch the picture and she'd make this rattling noise on the piano, that was like the horses coming... I don't suppose many kids can remember silent films.... My youngest brother couldn't read [the captions] and he used to say, "What they saying now?" "Oh, shut up!... If you went to school you could be able to know what they were saying, you'd be able to read!"...

Allied to the problem of the debt was the large number of people who had been made redundant in the area, it was eventually decided to allow them to use the cinema at a reduced price.

Unemployment and Hardship

By 1931, the cinema was facing a dual threat. On the one hand, the large and increasing number of unemployed was affecting attendances and consequently the takings; whilst the arrival of 'talkies' in surrounding cinemas led to a sharp drop in attendances at Oakdale. The decision was taken on 10th April 1931 to install audio equipment in the cinema, a move hastened by the fact that it was becoming increasingly difficult to obtain silent films. Two companies were considered for installing the sound equipment, namely Western Electric and the Gaumont Company; the latter being awarded the contract on 29th May. Four months later, 'silent films' returned when the loudspeaker failed!

They were forced into having to install talkies otherwise it would have gone down the drain. There's no doubt about that. But even with that, you see, once the novelty had worn off it became a question of which do you do - go to the pictures or buy a loaf of bread?

The community of Oakdale was, at this time, feeling the effects of the economic depression. Following a meeting between a deputation of the local unemployed and members of the Institute Committee it was agreed '...to allow them and their wives cinema admission at reduced prices...'.

There was always, as I can remember going to school, a lot of men outside the Institute. There'd be some up on the corner by the clock; there'd be some sitting on the seats; there'd be some standing in the doorway; there'd be some standing by the gate... Pennyless Corner my father always called it... My mother always used to say "Where are you going now then Ivor?" "Pennyless Corner for a hour."... They used to look so important, and yet they were poor people... There was nowhere else for them to go. There was no money for them to go to the pub - they went in there. My father would sit in there have a game of cards or he'd sit out on the seat and they'd talk. But I can always picture all those men sitting out or standing out by the front door.

The street corner next to the Institute became a popular gathering place for the men of the community. It was known locally as 'Pennyless Corner'.

The library was a particularly popular service to the local community and yet it was not able to obtain supplies of books from the County Library, even though there was no other public library in the vicinity. It was decided to pursue the matter through the County's Director of Education. In any case, the Institute's stock of books was growing and the room then being used as a library was both unsuitable and inadequate (this may have been the room which now houses the ladies' toilets). On 24 May 1932, it was agreed that the main committee room should be converted into a joint Library and Committee Room with shelves being installed, at a cost of £10. On November 22nd, the minutes record that an old Welsh Bible was presented to the library by the former Colliery Agent. At the same meeting, it was decided to convert the Telephone Room into the Caretaker's Office with glass panes being inserted into the door leading to the Reading Room so that the caretaker could supervise it.

The well-stocked shelves of the Library at Oakdale Institute, photographed in 1945.

I remember discovering the Library, I was fascinated by it. I suddenly walked in and there was all these books, and I was told I could have any book I wanted anytime, free of charge, because my father paid through the pit... I discovered books in the Library in the Institute and papers because of the Reading Room...I used to sit in the Reading Room for hours reading the papers... All sort of novels, history, you name it, classics - whatever was around, the Library had them. And it was a very good Library. I can picture it, I can smell it now. There was a particular smell about the Library and about the Reading Room. Whatever books you wanted you could have and they were there for you.

As the effects of unemployment grew, a Boot and Clothing Fund was established to provide boots and clothes for the children of the local unemployed. It was agreed that the New Hall should be made available for a Sunday evening concert to help raise money for the Fund. The Oakdale & District Distress Fund similarly received financial aid from the Institute.

By the 1934 AGM, over £6,000 was still outstanding on the various loans and attempts to increase income were constantly being thwarted by the effects of the recession. Whereas more people were now attending the cinema, income was down because so many of these were unemployed and taking advantage of the reduced entry charges. In fact, the Billiards Hall was the only part of the Institute that was showing a profit. Every room was in constant use, including the Lesser Hall which could be divided by means of a folding partition to provide separate meeting rooms.

It wasn't until about 1937-38 that things began to pick up... They tried to maintain the facilities to keep people's spirits up. During the depression - the early thirties - they did what they could. They were bound legally obviously to keep paying this loan back, and it must have been a job of robbing Peter to pay Paul all the time... But they kept it going somehow. It really was a struggle there's no doubt about that...

In 1935, it was decided that the interior of the Institute was in need of re-decoration. The Reading Room was to be spruced-up, as were the Games Room, Committee Room, lavatory, vestibule, staircase and landing. A new colour scheme was agreed upon, which would include a 'marble-effect' for the walls. The floor of the Lesser Hall was renewed and the cinema equipment in the New Hall upgraded and modernised.

Even though the library had only recently been re-located to one of the committee rooms, by late 1935 space for new books was already at a premium and the Committee was pressed for permission to convert one of the large committee rooms on the left of the foyer for use as a lending library. The other committee room was made available for use by the older (retired) men in the village between 10am and 4.45pm each day unless it was required for use by the Committee.

Oakdale Colliery Prize Band, photographed in 1937: one of the many groups which made use of the Institute's facilities.

When the Institute was running, they had various committees. They had the main committee, but then them committees was split up into sub committees. You had the picture house committee... and they would choose the films that was being put on. Then you had the library committee to choose the books and purchase books. And you had the games committee, with all the games that was taking place in there, like all the domino tournaments and cards and everything like that. All the tournaments was run by the games committee. One of the main things then of course was the finance committee. They met every week to produce the bills and the standing of the committee - you know, where the money was going. And of course we also had a cleaning committee. Now they went 'round every Tuesday. Went 'round the building into the picture house, and even had them running the fingers along the edges... There were some fussy men, if I can tell you.

Trustees and officials of the Oakdale Workmen's Institute, photographed in 1945, the year the loan from the Tredegar Iron and Coal Company was repaid.

The Second World War

In April 1938, ominous signs of the rising tensions in Europe were apparent when the local police requested the use of a room to hold classes on Air Raid Precautions, and by February of the following year, an ARP siren had been erected on the roof of the Picture House. At the same time, it was decided to remove the old partition from the Lesser Hall and to install it in the ground floor of the Picture House where it would act as a draught screen.

The Committee meanwhile made frequent approaches to the Central Welfare Fund for grant aid especially for moneys to help with improvements to the Institute and Picture House. The importance of grant aid became even more critical in October 1938 when Mr. W. D. Woolley, Managing Director of the Tredegar Iron Company wrote requesting repayment of all outstanding loans by the end of March the following year. The sum owing to the Company was still more than £6,000 and the Committee faced the daunting task of raising this amount in just five months. In spite of this, they nevertheless decided to proceed with erecting new iron railings on the boundary wall. The Miners' Welfare Fund meanwhile gave a grant of £400 to be spent on repairs and painting. The 'Welfare' also set out to investigate which Workmen's Halls and Institutes still had outstanding loans with a view to seeing how they could be assisted; the Committee at Oakdale must have awaited the outcome of their enquiries with interest.

In June 1939, the Lesser Hall was made available to the authorities for the reception of evacuees from London, whilst one of the other rooms was granted for use whenever the air raid siren sounded. The Lesser Hall was also used by the troops for P.T. instruction. The Institute was now being utilised to the full, probably for the first time since its opening in 1917; there were concerts, dances, meetings, lectures, ambulance and nursing classes. '...it [was] as if a new form of life [had] come to the place....'. The increased use being made of the Institute building during 1940 resulted in a surplus of more than £580. The repayments on the loan had been maintained and although the Company's original deadline had passed, they intimated that as long as repayments were kept up, they were prepared to be flexible and might even consider a rebate.

As long as they were able to pay the interest on the loan it was all right. And there were times when they could hardly do that... Funnily enough the saving of both the Picture House and the Institute was the war. If there hadn't been those two facilities in the village, I don't know what would have happened, because we were inundated you see with displaced persons, evacuees, an army camp, Bevin boys. And they all descended one after the other onto Oakdale. Before the war had ended they had paid back to the T.I.C. every copper they owed them and made a profit after struggling for years and years and years... In 1939 when we were waiting for Hitler to step ashore, the Home Guard was holding a dance! Greater faith hath no man!

Dances were held not solely for entertainment, they were also a means of raising money for the War effort. The War Services Fund made use of both the Lesser Hall and the Picture House for dances and concerts, and in October 1941, a dance was held to raise money to send medical supplies to Russia.

Relations were not always smooth between the Institute Committee and the ARP Wardens who manned the siren on the Picture House roof and had right of access through the building. The Institute's telephone was removed from the 'Siren Room' and replaced by an ARP telephone. References to the War Effort crop up regularly in the Institute's Minutes: a report given by one of the members at a meeting of the Anglo-Russian

The Lesser Hall, which occupied the whole of the first floor of the Institute, could accommodate more than 250 people. It was a popular venue for dances during the war years.

Movement; the playing of a recorded speech during a film show in the Picture House urging greater coal output to help the War Effort; a speech by a Naval Officer during the interval on behalf of the National Savings Movement; the showing of Ministry of Food slides, presumably on making the most of rationed food; and training films for the Home Guard and the Civil Defence Service. In September 1942, a room was granted for use as a Blood Transfusion Station whilst the former Library Room was used for registering Fire Guards and later for use as a Sector Point in case of a 'blitz'.

The announcement of the end of hostilities in Europe on Tuesday, 8th May (VE Day) was celebrated with a free matinee on Saturday, with all staff receiving double pay and two days' holiday. As part of the celebrations, lights and decorations were put up outside the Institute and a Peace Celebration Committee was formed in the village.

When the war ended the balcony was all lit up and decorated. Oh it was fantastic, I've never seen Oakdale look so nice, that night they put lights up all around it. That's what sticks in my mind...

After the War

By July 1945, a major milestone in the history of Oakdale Institute was in sight; the debt to the Tredegar Iron and Coal Company was about to be paid off. To mark the occasion, it was decided that a special ceremony be held at which the Deeds of the Properties would be handed over. Present were representatives of the Tredegar Iron and Coal Company, the Mortgagees, and Mr. Davies, District Organiser of the Miners' Welfare Fund. A Register, containing the names of all past members of the Institute was drawn up, with provision for the names of present and future board members to be added. A new Rule was adopted '...that before any Board Meeting ... the youngest sitting member should reverently take the Register from its place of keeping and place it on the table in front of the Chairman'.

It was decided to produce a book tracing the history of the Oakdale Institute from its inception to 1945, the book to include photographs of the current Committee as well as interior and exterior views of the Institute building and Picture House. Members were to be allowed free entry to the cinema for three nights and a free matinee for children on the Saturday afternoon '...for which event an outstanding film [was to be] booked'. Finally, a special gratuity was to be given to all members of the Institute staff to commemorate the event. In a Committee meeting held on 17th July 1945, Mr. R. Hopkins moved that the balance due to the Tredegar Iron and Coal Company be paid off. The fetters of the debt had at last been broken.

After the War, village life returned to a semblance of normality. Social life increased and wages improved to such an extent that many who had left during the War to seek work at the armament depots and factories at Glascoed and Caerwent, returned to work in the colliery. The Cinema and Institute were redecorated; an Amateur Dramatic Society was formed and an annual Drama Week was organised in which the leading Welsh drama companies participated. A silver cup was presented to the Institute by Ansells Brewery (who had purchased the Oakdale Hotel) to be awarded to the winning company.

OAKDALE WORKMEN'S LIBRARY AND INSTITUTE
Celebrating the Liquidation of "The Loans"
SOUVENIR PROGRAMME.
FOREWORD BY MR. W. A. PHILLIPS,
Chairman of the Board of Management.

"It has been said that Noah was the first man to provide indoor welfare comforts, but it is only in recent years that Miners' Institutes and Picture Houses have become important centres of educational and communal interests in the drab and irksome existence of the miner's everyday life.

"It is with gratitude and pride we think of the 'Noah's of Oakdale,' the pioneers—happily some are still with us—who saw visions and made their visions realities. The history of our Institution began 34 years ago, the first recorded meeting was held in April of 1912, inaugurated in the Sinkers Huts at the Oakdale Colliery, the earnest endeavours, the weekly contribution, the negotiated loan from the Tredegar Iron and Coal Co., Ltd., and then the erection of these beautiful buildings. Honoured be the memories of those courageous ones of the earliest days, who dared—and did. Now in the year 1946 the visions of those pioneers have become realities. These buildings, valued at £20,000, and all they entail, are now the sole property, free of all debt, of the Subscribers of Oakdale. We must not forget to pay tribute to the Boards of Management who have been responsible for the organisation, management and smooth running of our Institution.

"Your Board of Management has determined that this year of 1946 shall be known as our 'Celebration Year,' to celebrate the momentous occasion of being able to say that the whole of these hereditaments is now the sole property of our Subscribers, free from debt, and untrammelled with the ghastly nightmare of that monster 'The Loan' to the T.I.C.

"In conclusion, it is hoped that the future will bring our wives and daughters more to the fore in playing a more active part than hitherto in the life and work of the Institute. We can, I think now, look with some degree of right and expectation to the younger elements of our Subscribers to thoroughly interest themselves in what is now their own to have and to hold. They are inheritors of glorious traditions—traditions of sacrifice, of faith, of endeavour and of achievement.

"The vision now should be one of further achievement and progress, because in honour of the past pioneers, you dare not fail them, and with high resolution and faith inspired, your vision, too, should become a reality of accomplishment."

A performance of 'The Gift' by the Oakdale Dramatic Society, early 1950s.

A week's festival. Imagine that now, six plays per week.... They'd be queuing for tickets for hours and hours and hours. Queuing three and four abreast to get a ticket to go in for a week's performance, six nights. Wonderful!... The revenue it brought was tremendous... They'd have a sub-committee for selling tickets. Very well organised it's got to be to bring in the amount that they brought in... It was family involvement, because for instance my husband was helping with the sets then I roped him into acting as well. I was directing and sometimes writing the script and playing the principal part And my daughter [was] in the show as well. And who would come to see it? - my mother, my father, all my aunties, my cousins - so you had family involvement all down the line. Therefore your hall would be chock-a-block. Packed!

The Lesser Hall was also used for such varied uses as the occasional eisteddfod, wedding receptions and the annual May Queen or Rose Queen Festival:

The Rose Queen festival was held every year and the school teachers would join in. We'd have a day of sports... Johnny Lovell used to have lorries and he'd let us have a big lorry to put the queen on. He'd bring it up early in the morning, about half past six on a Saturday morning. And women would be bringing the carpets out from the house, and we'd put the sedan chair up there for her to sit in. They dressed the lorry up and then I'd have to take the queen then with her attendants down to Crumlin up to Cross Pen Maen down to Pontllanffraith and all round... Then at one o'clock we'd all meet by the 'Stute. The band would be out playing and then we'd parade all round the village ...the queen and her attendants and all the schools walking... Then we'd all go down to the welfare ground for sports and the maypole dancing. Harold Finch our M.P. would open the ceremony... And in the night after it was all over, we'd have a dance. Everybody would attend the dance up at the Institute in the Lesser Hall. We used to have a grand day...

For the first time since 1929 a large house-building programme was undertaken in the village with a council estate being built to the south of the village. A new church was built at the bottom of Central Avenue and a new primary school erected behind the Recreation Ground. The colliery was updated and modernised: electric winding gear replaced the steam-driven machinery in 1962, horses were replaced by 40″-wide conveyer belts and by the 1980s it had

The May Queen and her attendants, Oakdale, 1927.

The decorative archway over the main staircase of the Institute being removed from the building by members of the Museum of Welsh Life's re-erected buildings team, 1989

fundamental change in leisure activity. Many of the old societies and clubs dwindled in popularity and ceased functioning altogether. The Music Society and Dramatic Company were disbanded. The cinema projector was replaced by a 'bingo' caller and the annual Sunday School Whitsuntide walks and trips to the coast came to an end. In the words of Fred Hopkins, an Oakdale resident writing in the late 1960s, '...The upsurge of affluence in Oakdale [had] indeed taken its toll...'.

In a desperate attempt to reverse the trend of a dwindling membership, and against the advice of many Committee Members, the Institute applied for a grant from the Coal Industry Social Fund to convert the premises (including the cinema) to a modern licensed club, boasting as its attractions five bars and a colour television set! The Library was closed and the books dispersed when a branch of the County Library opened in the village in 1967.

become one of the most modern, efficient and productive mines in South Wales. Its future seemed secure into the next millennium, but this was not to be. In 1989, as part of a wholesale rationalisation programme carried out by British Coal, Oakdale, along with virtually every remaining pit in South Wales, was forced to close.

The period from the mid-1950s to 1970 saw a marked and fundamental change in village life in Oakdale as elsewhere. The arrival of popular television and the increase in car-ownership led to a dramatic and

They put bars in there... And that was the worse thing that ever happened to that place. They had a bar where the reading room used to be; they had a bar down in the billiard hall; they had a bar upstairs in the dance hall... It wasn't the same place as I remember when I was growing up. You learnt to respect those sort of places... but when it went into a pub, I think that was the downfall of the Institute.

In recent years new, private houses were built nearby. Even though new work has come into the area since the closure of the pit and even though some activities, such as the Rugby Club, Youth Choir and Silver Band, have witnessed a revival of interest, the old Institute and Cinema were unable to recover their former glory. In 1987, they closed their doors for the last time and the buildings were acquired by Islwyn Borough Council. Plans were made for their demolition in order that the site could be developed for sheltered housing. Coincidentally, this happened at a time when the Museum of Welsh Life (then the Welsh Folk Museum) was actively looking for a public hall for re-erection at St. Fagans. In 1989, the Institute building was dismantled and transported to the Museum. The Cinema was not acquired as it was considered to be too large for the proposed site. Despite its decline, the removal of the Institute has left Oakdale's older generation with mixed feelings:

It was really a question of which do you need the most: an old people's residence for the ageing population or a derelict community centre you can't afford anyway... The fact that St Fagans were very pleased to have the chance to take it and to rebuild it faithfully was the main thing... I mean they numbered every stone, didn't they, when they took it away. But it was quite a sad moment all the same when you see something which is almost the heart of the village being torn away...

...How everything comes flooding back to you! I could hear all these men that I knew years ago whilst I was a kid.... I said "Do you know, you're talking to me now, and I can hear old Harry Chapman shouting up in there. I can hear them arguing over there - somebody had put a wrong domino down." And I was crying, I was crying like the rain...

Rebuilding work commenced in 1992 and the building was opened to the public on Saturday, 14 October 1995. The Opening Ceremony was performed by Rt. Hon. Neil Kinnock, European Commissioner for Transport, formerly leader of the Labour Party and MP for the constituency of Bedwellty within which Oakdale was situated.

Acknowledgements

We are indebted to many people for their co-operation in preparing this publication, especially those who entrusted us with family photographs and who agreed to the recorded interviews which bring the text to life.

We would particularly like to acknowledge the assistance, advice and information given by the following:

Peter Bennett, Welsh Industrial and Maritime Museum

Rev. Tom Davies and Mrs Barbara Davies, Cardiff, South Glamorgan

Michael K. Garland, Newport, Isle of Wight

Gwent Record Office

Tony Hadland, photographer, National Museums and Galleries of Wales

Mr and Mrs Glyn Hughes, Oakdale, Gwent

David Jones, Oakdale, Gwent

Joanne Keenan, South Wales Miners' Library, Swansea, West Glamorgan

Mrs Rosalie Lewis, Tredegar, Gwent

Jack Morris, Blackwood, Gwent

George Page and Mrs Peggy Page, Oakdale, Gwent

South Wales Miners' Museum, Afan Argoed, West Glamorgan

Neville Tallis, Swansea, West Glamorgan

Ralph Thomas and Mrs Kathleen Thomas, Penmaen, Gwent

Roy Thomas, Caerphilly, Mid Glamorgan

Kenneth Tiley, Cwmcarn, Gwent

Mrs Peggy Witcombe, Oakdale, Gwent

Further Reading

John Benson, *British Coalminers in the Nineteenth Century*, Gill & Macmillan, 1980

R. Page Arnot, *South Wales Miners*, Unwin, 1967

George H. Hoare (ed.), *The History of the Oakdale Institute*, 1946

Craig Jones, *The Miners' Institutes, Workmen's Halls and Welfare Halls of South Wales*, unpublished Ph.D. thesis, Polytechnic of Wales, 1990

G. M. Clarke, *The Plight of Miners' Halls and Institutes in South Wales*, unpublished Ph.D. thesis, Bristol Polytechnic, 1989

Neil Sumner, *The Role of Workmen's Institutes in the Development of Community in the South Wales Coalfield 1880-1920*, unpublished M.A. thesis, Sunderland Polytechnic, 1991

Hywel Francis, 'Workers' Libraries: the Origins of the South Wales Miners' Library' *History Workshop: a Journal of Socialist Historians*, vol 2, 1976, pp 183-203

Fred Hopkins, *Sixty Years at Oakdale Colliery*, Gwent County Library, 1980

Ralph Thomas, *Oakdale: The Model Village*, Village Publishing, Cwmbran, 1986